STAR SCENE CONFIDENTIAL

School COOL

By Michael Anne Johns

SCHOLASTIC INC.

New York   Toronto   London   Auckland

Sydney   Mexico City   New Delhi   Hong Kong

ISBN-10: 0-545-15901-6
ISBN-13: 978-0-545-15901-2

© 2009 by Scholastic Inc.

Published by Scholastic Inc.
SCHOLASTIC and associated logos are trademarks and/or registered trademarks of Scholastic Inc.

12 11 10 9 8 7 6 5 4 3 2 1   9 10 11 12 13 14/0

Designed by Deena Fleming and Two Red Shoes Design
Printed in the U.S.A.
First printing, September 2009

CONTENTS!

INTRODUCTION!

It's that time of year again. The bathing suits, surfboards, and summer memories are put on the back shelf. Now it's all about dealing with new schools, new classes, new friends, new . . . new . . . new!

It can be a little bit overwhelming, but the good thing about September is that it soon turns into October, and everything becomes familiar again! That's true for everyone — even those superstars who are on posters on your bedroom wall. Believe it or not, Zac Efron, the JoBros, Miley Cyrus, Robert Pattinson, Chelsea Staub, and many more all went through the "school blues" at one time or another. And in the end, the blues turned into blue skies.

Check out the celebrity school tales on the following pages. You might get a laugh or two and you may even recognize yourself somewhere along the line!

JONAS BROTHERS

The School Bus Tour

With their incredible rise to success, it seems like a lifetime ago that Nick, Kevin, and Joe Jonas were typical school guys back in Wyckoff, NJ. But there was a time the Jonas brothers were concerned about homework and tests. Concert tours, TV shows, and movies were just a dream away!

So what were they like in school? Let's ask them. . . .

Cool Kevin

"I was a total nerd," claims Kevin. "Everyone used to make fun of me. I had extremely large, Spock-like ears growing up. I had to grow into my ears. I had glasses, and no one would let me in their band. . . . I was bullied. I was the oddball because I liked music. [Eventually] I found a group of friends who were all into fashion and music. . . . It was kind of funny. But I guess it worked out, so I'm fine!"

Hmmm, looks like it did!

KEVIN'S KICKS

- "I love bowling. I was a varsity bowler in high school."
- Kevin's favorite school subject was history — "I understand it."
- Kevin's math tip — "Work hard, and you will get it right sooner or later."
- The first book Kevin ever read? *Disney's Thumper.*
- Chemistry is Kevin's favorite science subject. Of course, there was the time "I blew up silver nitrate all over the room!"
- Kevin's favorite thing about school was the "constant interaction with others."

Just Joe

When the Jonas Brothers appeared on MTV's music show *FNMTV* in July 2008, they were celebrating more than the success of their CD, concert tour, and announcement of their TV series *JONAS*. Joe had just accomplished something big. "A big congratulations to Joe," Kevin told the Los Angeles crowd. "He just graduated from high school. It happened yesterday, so it's a big deal!"

When Joe took the microphone, he laughed. "I haven't heard from the school yet, but I'm officially done with the work!"

At that moment, school was "yesterday," and Joe was totally looking forward to all his tomorrows. But when he was asked about a memorable time back in school, he paused for a second and smiled. "Growing up, I was always a weird kid," he said. "I used to think it was cool to go to bed and pretend to fall asleep, and then get up and change into my school clothes for the next day and sleep in them. I don't know why! I guess I wanted to be prepared for the next morning."

Guess he didn't want to be late for the first bell at school!

JOE'S JOYS

- Joe's favorite class was "recess!"
- Joe's favorite teacher — "My third grade teacher. I had a crush on her."
- The first book Joe read was a Dr. Seuss story.
- Joe's biggest science disaster — "I once tried to make a volcano . . . it didn't work!"
- His most embarrassing moment in school — "Getting called to the principal's office the first day of school."

Nick's Nook

"I was doing Broadway shows [when I was in middle school], and they didn't get it," recalls Nick about his classmates. "I didn't even want to talk to them about it, because they weren't excited for me."

Like his brothers, Nick was teased a bit at school. Kevin was made fun of because of his ears. Joe says, "Kids who I didn't like would make fun of my name and call me 'JJ Jonas!' I had to hear it every day at school!" But Kevin and Joe set a good example to Nick and told him not to pay attention to the mean kids. Nick says he learned the lesson well. Now he advises, "You've got to avoid situations that make you uncomfortable." And he adds, "Don't get mad at yourself. It's not your fault. It's just that everyone else is [acting] stupid. That's the truth!"

That's the spirit!

NICK'S PICKS

- Nick's favorite subject is spelling — "I'm pretty good at it."
- The first book Nick ever read was *The Magic School Bus*.
- Nick's favorite science subject is geology.
- Nick is fascinated by the history of the French Revolution.

MILEY CYRUS

School Memories

When Miley looks back at her days as a "regular" kid in Tennessee, it seems like a lifetime ago. In many ways it is. The last time Miley hit the schoolhouse and rushed to class at the sound of the bell was when she was in sixth grade. Once she moved to Los Angeles to pursue her career, she started homeschooling and being tutored on the set of *Hannah Montana* or on the road during her concert tours. That was a major change for Miley, and one she had to adjust to. The studying part wasn't too bad — she's kept her grade average at the A/B level and is taking some advanced classes. But according to Miley, the hard part of leaving the classroom was leaving her friends.

"I miss the social part, for sure," Miley admits when questioned about the things she had to give up for fame and fortune. When she moved to Hollywood, Miley recalls, "It was bittersweet." Sure, she headed for a whole new adventure, but she also left her lifelong friends and activities that she loved. "I hung out with a small group of friends I've known all my life because I went to the same school my whole life," she explains.

Miley remembers when the day of the move came. She and her childhood friend, Lesley, "were crying all day long. At the end of the day, my mom picked me up. I was like, 'Mom, I don't want to leave!'"

But leave she did, and the rest is history. Miley still has the memories of her school days. Here are a few of them . . .

First Date-Mate

"My very first date was in kindergarten. It was stupid. It was with one of my best friends. We went and saw the *Muppet Babies* in 3D. I thought it was so awesome."

Go Cowboys!

Miley started cheerleading when she was six years old — her team was called the Cowboys. In middle school, Miley's cheerleading squad was a main part of her life. "The training was pretty harsh, but it was so worth it once you were on stage and getting trophies."

Ms. Competitive

Even back in first grade, Miley was interested in performing — and sometimes it became competitive. "My little boyfriend in first grade was going to do the talent show, too, and I was like, 'Oh, no, it's going down.' So I broke up with him because he was going to be in the talent show. I thought if he really liked me, he should just let me win, and of course, he wouldn't let me win. I was really mean like that!"

MUST-KNOW MILEY

- Miley's favorite subject is math — "I love a good challenge."
- Miley's favorite teacher was Ms. Sevier from second grade.
- Miley's favorite book when she was little was *Little Ballerina*.
- The first book Miley read was *Goodnight Moon*.
- Miley's favorite author is Roald Dahl.
- Miley's most embarrassing moment in school was the day . . . "I cut off a pair of jeans to capris, and at lunch they split all the way up to the side of my hip bone!"
- Miley's friend used to tease her for "snorting when I laugh."

ZAC EFRON

Life Is A High School Musical

When you think of Zac Efron, you almost automatically think High School — *High School Musical 1, 2,* and *3* . . . *Hairspray* . . . *17 Again*. But Zac is the first one to tell you that when he was back in school, he was anything but the Big Man on Campus!

"Troy from *HSM* is a cool guy," Zac observes. "He has this confidence that I didn't have in high school. I wouldn't say that I was a geek, but I was never one of the cool kids. I was too focused on school, and I was kind of known as one of the theater kids around town. I was also the shortest kid! I was really short and skinny until I got bigger in my junior year, and I had a huge gap in my front teeth! I got teased about that gap more than anything else."

Of course, Zac wasn't exactly a "lone wolf" in school. He had a lot of friends. "I didn't belong to any one clique," he says. "In high school, I had friends who were sort of like everywhere. I did it by class — I had my drama friends. I had friends who were stars of the basketball team. I had another friend who just played computer games all day. The thing is, you learn so much by talking to different people at school."

Little did he know that his high school days would be good training for his future film roles!

Zac Attack

- Zac's favorite subject was English.
- Zac's #1 math tip — "A calculator is your best friend!"
- Biology was Zac's favorite science subject.
- Science disaster — "I spilled sulfuric acid on my notebook. My entire year's notes melted instantly!"
- Zac's favorite thing about school? "Seeing my friends."
- Zac's least favorite things about school were "Waking up in the morning

EMILY OSMENT

The Surprise

The *Hannah Montana* costar doesn't mind admitting when she is wrong — especially when it comes to misunderstandings with friends. When Emily is not taping *Hannah Montana* or filming a movie, she goes to a private high school, and she has close friends she's practically grown up with. She will never forget the day she got into a major fight with her best friend at school.

"It was for an unbelievably stupid reason," Emily remembers. "I felt like my friends were keeping something from me, and I got really mad instead of being mature and thinking, 'Oh, it's a secret, and I don't care.' I felt something was wrong. Everybody I talked to was avoiding me, and I got really mad at my best friend because I knew she knew everything. Turns out they were throwing a surprise party for me, and she was the one who threw the party! I wish I could do that over and ignore everything."

Luckily, friendship overcame all the hurt feelings and mix-ups. "There were lots of tears and fighting that day, but we got through it," Emily sighs. "A friend is someone who is always there for you, who you can enjoy being with, who's got your back, and who you can have a lot of fun with."

Emily learned her lesson and says she isn't so quick to react now — especially when it comes to friends she really loves and trusts!

EMILY EXTRAS

- Emily's favorite author is Rodman Philbrick.
- Emily's favorite book series is *The Uglies*.
- Emily's favorite book is *Lord of the Flies*.
- Emily studies Spanish at school.
- Emily's favorite historical era is the Renaissance—"for the clothes!"
- Emily's favorite high school memory is "Getting asked to Homecoming and having the boy give me a big card in front of everyone!"

BOOK-NOOK READING ROOM

Read, baby, read! That's the chant from your favorite celebrities. Check out what they say about the books they love and why reading is important . . . and fun!

Debby Ryan
(Suite Life on Deck)

"I'm in the middle of reading *Princess of Gossip* by Sabrina Bryan, and I love it. I cannot put it down. And I [love] the *Princess Diaries* series. I also love *Hamlet*. I can never get enough of that. I love Shakespeare. . . . [Reading] just broadens your horizons. I love it."

Emma Roberts
(The Winning Season)

"I'm reading *The Glass Castle* at the moment. Everyone recommended it to me. I picked it up at the airport, and I can't put it down. . . . I read every single *Gossip Girl* book there was. When I was really younger, I read the *Junie B. Jones* series. My sister reads them now. . . . Reading is important because it fills your imagination and builds your vocabulary. I know it helped me a lot in recognizing what words mean. Instead of watching TV in your free time, it's great to pick up a book."

Josh Henderson
(Journey to the Center of the Earth)

"I had heard of *Journey to the Center of the Earth* before [the movie], but I hadn't read it. When we were filming, [the book] was always on the set, so I kind of looked through it. . . . I like *The Catcher in the Rye* — that kind of story. *To Kill a Mockingbird*."

Abigail Breslin
(Kit Kittredge: An American Girl)

"I love *Anne of Green Gables* — it's one of my favorite books. I just love Anne because she's so funny, and she's just crazy. She names everything. It's funny. I would recommend the book because it's just a fun book to read, and Anne sort of overcomes all her little faults."

Sabrina Bryan
(The Cheetah Girls)

"One of my favorite books when I was younger was *Matilda*. I like magic and I like mysteries. Right now I'm hooked on J.D. Robb books — it's Nora Roberts under a different name. They're set in the future."

Dakota Fanning
(The Secret Life of Bees)

"I think probably *Charlotte's Web* is my favorite children's book, and my favorite adult book is *The Secret Life of Bees* — they are so heartfelt, and so touching and moving to read. And I think they're the kind of books you can read over and over again at any stage of your life."

Selena Gomez
(Wizards of Waverly Place)

"My favorite book when I was little was *The Wonderful Wizard of Oz*. . . . My mom read that book to me, and then I read it over and over. I loved Dorothy and I loved the characters and I have the movie. I have no idea why, but I just loved that book."

Jennifer Stone
(Wizards of Waverly Place)

"I'm reading *The Picture of Dorian Gray* by Oscar Wilde. I really like it. I've come to find that Jane Austen and Oscar Wilde are the two classic writers that are easy to understand. I love reading — it's an escape from reality. If you're having a bad day, you can grab a book and read and go into a whole different world. It's a great way to escape."

Miranda Cosgrove (*iCarly*)

"I read *The Catcher in the Rye*, and it's really good. I thought it was going to be one of those boring books, but it's not boring at all. And I recently read *To Kill a Mockingbird*, and it was really cool too."

Vincent Martella
(*Everybody Hates Chris*)

"I just finished *All Quiet on the Western Front*. It's so brilliant. I love that book. It wasn't one I had to read for class, but it was on the list."

Jennette McCurdy (*iCarly*)

"I'm reading the Twilight series. I just read *Twilight, New Moon* and I'm halfway through *Eclipse,* and I'm loving it so much."

FIRST-DAY MEMORIES

First-day jitters? Butterflies in the stomach? These are universal experiences — even your faves went through them! Read on. . .

Demi Lovato
(Sonny With a Chance)

"I was always a tomboy and hung out with the guys in fifth grade, so when I went to junior high for the first day, I wore a little dress or a skirt. I wore make-up, and I did my hair and everyone looked at me like, 'Who's that?' It was cool. I liked it."

Nicole Anderson (JONAS)

"My worst first day of school was moving to a new school and not knowing anybody. I was shy and really didn't put myself out there. My dad was in the Navy, so we moved a lot, but as I got older, it got easier and I learned it never hurts to meet new people."

Jared Padalecki
(Supernatural)

"I never slept before the first day of school. I wasn't nervous, but it was anticipation and [I was] sad that the summer was over, but excited about the first day of school."

David Henrie
(Wizards of Waverly Place)

"I remember I came back to school in Arizona after missing the first few weeks. I'd been in California, so I had all these cool new clothes. I was so different from everyone else, and it was cool because I was a real trendsetter. It was great."

Brenda Song
(Suite Life on Deck)

"In fourth grade, all three of my best friends were in my class, and I had the most amazing teacher. I knew it was going to be a great year."

19

Mitchel Musso
(Hannah Montana)

"I loved every first day of school, especially in sixth grade. Now that I'm out of it and doing homeschool, I miss it a lot. I loved school."

Dustin Milligan
(90210)

"I've always had pretty good first days. I always tried to get that one good outfit and that one awesome binder and awesome new calculator."

Kay Panabaker (Fame)

"My best first day was in the fourth grade. We'd just moved to this new city, and I had to walk to school as opposed to riding the bus and I loved it. I got to meet new friends before I actually got to school."

Madison Pettis
(Cory in the House)

"I [had] just started fifth grade at a new school, and I was so nervous because everyone had their own little cliques and had already been friends since kindergarten. But I had five hundred kids surrounding me saying, 'You're the girl from *Cory in the House*!' It was kind of crazy, but now I'm just Madison."

Nathan Kress
(iCarly)

"I remember walking into kindergarten. I had freaked out the night before. I was crying, 'I'm going to get creamed.' I thought it was a place where kids get beat up. But I walked into school and said, 'This is so cool!'"

GO TO THE HEAD OF THE CLASS

What's your fave subject? English? Math? Lunch? See if you share the same picks with Hollywood's hotties!

Demi Lovato
(Camp Rock, Sonny With a Chance)

"Math is my favorite subject because you can always find an answer to a problem. There is always an explanation. I love to solve things."

Blake Lively
(Gossip Girl)

"English and math are my favorite subjects. It's so exciting to solve problems. It's thrilling. I was very involved in extracurricular [programs] as well. I was in Show Choir. We were number one in the nation. That was one of my biggest passions."

Mark Indelicato
(Ugly Betty)

"My favorite subject is European history — Spain, Rome, all that."

Sterling Beaumon
(Mostly Ghostly)

"What is my favorite subject? That's a toughie. I'm going to have to go with math. It's one of my harder subjects, but it's one of the funnest. Because I also want to be an architect when I grow up, if I can, and I know that being an architect takes a lot of math."

Selena Gomez
(Wizards of Waverly Place)

"Favorite subject? Probably science — at the moment. I'm studying physical science: the layers of the Earth and everything. It's fascinating to learn about our Earth. I just think it's fun to learn stuff like that."

Carter Jenkins
(They Came From Upstairs)

"Math is my favorite subject, though I [began] liking it a little bit less when it got complicated. You know . . . they put letters in there. I don't know why they did that. I was used to just numbers. It confused me. When I started getting into higher math, it actually threw me for a little bit . . . but when I started to get it, I actually found it to be kind of fun."

Taylor Lautner
(Twilight)

"I liked math more in junior high than high school. I enjoy more creative classes versus the analytical classes, so my favorite class is English."

Dakota Fanning
(The Secret Life of Bees)

"I really love English; history was definitely a challenge this year, but I feel like I learned a lot. I had a great teacher. Also photography — that was a lot of fun."

Reggie Bush
(NFL's New Orleans Saints)

went to Helix Charter High in La Mesa, CA, and his favorite class was sports medicine. His fave high school memory was "playing football." Reggie was also in the chess club.

LOCKER ROOM JOCKS

Ben Roethlisberger
(NFL's Pittsburgh Steelers)

went to Findlay High in Findlay, OH, and in his yearbook he was voted as having the "Ugliest Car." Ben also played basketball for his school and was named Great Lakes League Player of the Year.

Tony Romo
(NFL's Dallas Cowboys)

went to Burlington High in Burlington, WI, and played on the golf team. After graduation he tried to qualify for the U.S. Open three times — he never made it.

ROBERT PATTINSON

FROM WIZARD TO VAMPIRE

We first caught a glimpse of British cutey Robert Pattinson as Cedric Diggory in *Harry Potter and the Goblet of Fire*. He definitely has what it takes to be a heartthrob star! You know, talent, looks, and determination. But bet you didn't know that the one quality Robert values the most is imagination! And he feels the best way to stretch the imagination is reading!

Robert fondly remembers reading as a little boy, especially one book — "I used to love this book called *The Phantom Tollbooth*. I absolutely loved that. There is also [a series] similar to Harry Potter called Beaver Towers. My teacher used to read them in class when I was like, I don't remember how old I was, but I was pretty young. But I still remember them like it was yesterday. I love children's books. I kind of prefer them to adult's books basically. A well-written children's book is so much more satisfying. . . . I really like fantasy stuff, but I don't like fantasy written for adults unless it is really, really well-written. It just sort of complicates a simple idea."

ROBERT 411

- Robert's dream job is "being a pianist."
- Robert says his worst habit is "speaking too much."
- Robert loves to watch the movie *Pippi Longstocking*.

KRISTEN STEWART

School Notes

Twilight's Bella, Kristen Stewart, is a born-and-bred Californian, and was actually brought up in a showbiz family. Her dad, John Stewart (not the comedian Jon Stewart!) is a TV producer, and her mom, Jules, is a screenwriter, so it isn't too surprising Kristen chose acting as a career. She has appeared in films such as *What Just Happened, Into the Wild, Zathura, Catch That Kid, Panic Room*, and of course, *Twilight*. Those are just a few of the films she has appeared in.

The funny thing is that it wasn't her parents' connection to showbiz that led Kristen into acting . . . it was school!

"I've always been pretty shy," Kristen reveals. "When I was in the fourth and fifth grade, I think I was like eleven, everyone had to participate in this school play. And there were talent scouts there, and they called my house and they were like, 'Well, you know, we basically find kids and send them out, and have meetings with agents to see if they might get started in the business.' At first we weren't interested because my whole family is in the business, so we were like 'That's weird, no thanks.' And they called back a couple of times, and I was like, 'Well, it's worth a try.' So, it worked out."

As successful as 19-year-old Kristen is as an actress, she is totally willing to take a break and finish her education. "Acting is definitely not all I want to do," she explains. "It's not the most intellectually stimulating thing that you can possibly do. I want to go to college. I don't want to miss that. I want to be a writer. I think that'd be awesome."

And guess who Kristen's first "teacher" was — *Twilight* author Stephenie Meyer. During the filming of *Twilight*, Stephenie went to the set a couple of times, and Kristen got the opportunity to speak with her. "We got along well. She's a warm person. But I didn't speak to her about my character or the books. I did ask her how she got to write them and what other kinds of books she likes."

Not a bad "Introduction to Literature 101"!

STEWART STUFF

* Kristen wants to major in literature in college.
* Kristen is writing screenplays.
* Kristen says she's known most of her friends since kindergarten. "Once everything starts happening, you never really know who's really being your friend," she explains about "new" friends.

KEKE PALMER

This Bee-Girl Is A True A-Student!

"I was a pretty good speller before the movie *Akeelah and the Bee*," admits Keke Palmer. "But now I'm *very* good!"

Not only did her spelling skills excel since the box-office biggie, but Keke also became a teen queen out Hollywood way. In 2008, Nickelodeon introduced Keke in her very own sitcom, *True Jackson, VP*. As a teenaged vice president at a fashion-design company, Keke's *True Jackson* proves that if you work hard and are willing to take chances, your dreams might come true.

As much fun as it is playing True for Keke, she always stresses "education is everything" in her interviews. Here are some of her tips on being a top student:

ASK FOR HELP...

"I have great memorization skills, so when I look at my script, I only have to see it two or three times, and I get it. But my mom also helps me. Other kids who don't have that quality can just keep studying or do some of the things that [the real-life] Akeelah did. She had her mom help her; her teacher helped, too. When she had problems with her teacher, she went to her friends; she went to her community; she went to the homeless guy down the street, and he helped. You can always ask for help . . . but you should always depend on yourself, too."

Read, read, read . . .

"I like reading, and I like learning new words and definitions. One of my favorite books is *A Wrinkle in Time* — I read that even when I didn't have to read it for school. I love adventure books like Harry Potter . . . . My all-time favorite book is *Everlost* by Neal Shusterman. It's a magical book, one of those fantasies. I thought it was so cool. I hope they make it into a movie, because it's such a cool book."

DID YOU KNOW?

- Keke would love to play Jo if they ever remake *Little Women*.
- Keke's favorite hobby is "talking on the phone."
- Keke's real name is Lauren Palmer; her older sister nicknamed her "Keke."

HALLWAY HORRORS

Have you ever been caught passing a note in class? Or tripped in front of your secret crush? Well, have no fear — even your favorite stars had days they hit the top of the blush-o-meter!

Carter Jenkins
(They Came From Upstairs)

"Yeah, I went to private school for most of my elementary school years. I remember one time I had these shorts. I hadn't done my laundry in a while — I was backed up on laundry. I had these shorts and maybe they were a little small. It was always a big thing for me that the shorts couldn't come above the knees. The shorts had to go below the knees because that's what is cool, that's what basketball players wore. And I had these shorts that went above the knees, and I was miserable that whole day. I tried to pull my pants down lower so they would go down, but that was too low. I remember that day a lot. And I saw this girl who was, like, in eighth grade — I was maybe in third or fourth grade. She walked by me. *Eighth grade!* I was horrified because my pants came above my knees."

Emily Osment
(Hannah Montana)

"The day before the first day of ninth grade, I was at a party and I got hit in the head by a Frisbee. I had a scar on my face for the first two weeks of school. That's how I met everyone in ninth grade."

Madison Davenport
(Kit Kittredge: An American Girl)

"Last year, after I dyed my hair brown for Kit Kittredge, everyone was like, 'Who's the foreign exchange student?' I was like, 'It's me — Madison. I was here last year!'"

Selena Gomez
(Wizards of Waverly Place)

"Wow. I probably have many. I'm a klutz, so I trip and fall and knock over things all the time. More than likely, that's the most embarrassing thing. I've actually tripped through my friend's books into a trash can. So everyone knows me as the klutz when I went to school. I'm just a klutz, so I trip a lot."

Sterling Beaumon
(Mostly Ghostly)

"Oh, oh. I have one. Just yesterday actually, I was walking and texting on my phone — now, kids, never walk and text on your phone because it is not a smart idea. You'll probably end up tripping and smashing your face on a bench like I did."

Demi Lovato
(Sonny With a Chance)

"[One of the football players at school] was really cute. But I don't think he ever looked at me."

One day her teacher heard Demi talking about the boy, and "[the teacher] brings him into the room and tells him someone was just talking about him. 'Someone here has a crush on you,' my teacher said. And at this point, I was so embarrassed. And [the guy] said, 'Oh really? Who is it?' And everyone points to me! I was just sinking in my chair, and I was like, 'Hi?'"

Ana Maria Perez de Tagle (*Camp Rock*)

"It was the first day of freshman year. I was walking down the steps and noticed a very cute boy. I was trying to impress him by walking really slowly in heels and flirting — and then I fell really hard! Everyone found out and made fun of me for the rest of the year."

Cole Sprouse
(*Suite Life on Deck*)

"Embarrassed? At school? I remember being really nervous because [I was going to] a new school, and it was the first day and a bird pooped down my back!"

SCHOOL SURVIVAL GUIDE

Check out how these stars overcame their personal obstacles — maybe their solutions can help you!

David Archuleta

(American Idol)

FRIENDSHIP: "In eighth grade, I was a hermit. I wasn't sociable. I didn't like talking to people. People would try talking to me, and I was like, 'Ugh!' I just shut everybody out."

Until . . . David met his sister's friend Jessie. "I started hanging out with her, and it totally changed me. She was really talkative, so it opened me up. She helped me a lot!"

JoJo

CLASS OUTCAST: "[My friends] all turned on me [in high school]. I was left alone. I cried! I tried to talk to them, but they didn't want to and would gossip about me behind my back. My mom told me just to focus on school. I was afraid to go to class at times. I would eat lunch in my counselor's office."

Selena Gomez
(Wizards of Waverly Place)

TRUE TO YOU: "Just expressing yourself and being true to yourself means more than anything! It's likely that other people have a talent that they're afraid of showing as well. I mean, I got made fun of because I was in *Barney*! Just know that, at the end of the day, you *will* be okay."

Pete Wentz
(Fall Out Boy)

NERD HERD: "I was an outsider in school, but if I knew then what I know now, I would have stopped being an underachiever and stopped worrying about living up to anyone's [expectations]. I probably would have paid more attention and done better. Once you get out of high school, things change. Too many people in high school focus on what they think is going to last for the rest of their lives. You have to realize that just because you're a nerd doesn't mean you're going to be one forever."

Fergie

TEASE-A-RAMA: "I got made fun of for being on the show *Kids Incorporated*. It hurt my feelings! I was sensitive about what people said about me because I wanted to be liked. I have learned to develop who I am. I have my opinion, and those people have their opinion. I try not to let all of that affect me. You can't please everybody!"

CHELSEA STAUB

SHE'S NO BRATZ!

Bratz, Minutemen, and now *JONAS* — Chelsea Staub knows how to pick the movies and TV shows she stars in! The Arizona-born actress attended regular school even though she had started acting when she was eight years old. In fact, she's the first to tell everyone, "I loved school!"

She attended Saguaro High School in Phoenix and was even elected class president. "I loved student government," she recalls. "I was able to have a voice for all the students. And I got a battle of the bands started at my school. It was fun to decorate for dances and really feel like you were a part of it, as opposed to just kind of wandering the halls."

So when Chelsea had to make the decision of taking the next step in her career and moving to Los Angeles, she also had to leave the school she loved and begin homeschooling. It was a hard decision, but she had to do it.

But it wasn't only school that was hard to leave — it was also her friends. She soon learned the true importance of friendship.

"You have to work to keep your friendships alive," she says. "[When you move, your friends] don't just hang around, and people move on with their lives. I think a lot of people, when I would go away, thought that everyone else was just frozen in time and when I came back, we would pick up right where we left off. The lesson I learned is that I work really hard to keep my friendships going. We talk on the phone when I'm out of town . . . we write letters. I think when you find those people, you have to fight to hang on to them, because they're rare and amazing."

CHELSEA FACTS

- Chelsea is a huge fan of the Twilight book series — "It's the book I'm saying, 'Oh my gosh, have you read this? You've got to read this!'"
- Chelsea's favorite children's book was *Rainbow Fish*.
- Chelsea would love to play "Bella" from the Twilight series — "But I think I missed that," she laughs.

VICTORIA JUSTICE

School Day Q&A

Nickelodeon's newest star, Victoria Justice — from *Zoey 101*, *Spectacular!*, and her own upcoming sitcom — takes a pop quiz all about school!

DO YOU LIKE TO READ?

Victoria: Yes, I love to read; I've been reading all my life. [If] my friends ask to hang out, and if I'm not feeling up to it, I'll just sit home and read a good book. Reading just takes you to another world, and it's a really good way to expand your vocabulary and learn. I just love reading — it's awesome.

WHAT THREE BOOKS WOULD YOU RECOMMEND TO A FRIEND?

Victoria: OK, let's see . . . *Twilight*, definitely. I would also recommend *Esperanza Rising*. I remember that I loved it. And what's another book that I really liked? Hmm . . . oh, it's this book called *A Great and Terrible Beauty* by Libba Bray, and it's really good.

DO YOU REMEMBER YOUR BEST FIRST DAY OF SCHOOL?

Victoria: Hmm . . . I don't know. I remember that my first day of middle school was amazing, because all of my friends from elementary school were going to that middle school. So we all just saw each other on the first day and ran up to each other, and we just felt like such grown-ups because we were in middle school now! We had an awesome time, going up to random people and introducing ourselves, and we didn't have a care in the world. [Laughs] It was a lot of fun; that was a fun day.

DO YOU REMEMBER A REALLY EMBARRASSING MOMENT IN SCHOOL?

Victoria: I've had so many embarrassing moments it's hard to think of one. Let's see, embarrassing moment at school . . . oh, I remember one time, at my high school everyone eats on this area called the quad, and it's kind of like grassy, and it has a lot of mud and stuff [on rainy days]. And one day, it was really muddy and really wet on the quad. But for some reason, I still wanted to eat on the quad. So I kept walking, and in front of everyone, I stepped on a patch of mud and I slipped and I fell on my butt! Everyone on the quad looked at me, and it was really embarrassing.

WAIT . . . THERE'S ONE MORE!

"One time I was walking in school, and a bird swooped down and started following me. I started running and screaming that the bird was attacking me. People just started to laugh. It was actually pretty funny. Embarrassing, but funny!"

IS IT HARD TO JUGGLE WORK AND SCHOOL?

Victoria: Sometimes it's difficult. I get homework every night, and when you have an audition the next day, you need to work on that, too. I'm such a perfectionist that I'm always going for those straight A's, and I also want to feel that I gave the audition my all. I try to do my best at both.

DID YOU EVER PARTICIPATE IN SPELLING BEES?

Victoria: Yes! In elementary school I made it to the finals in our fifth grade spelling bee. I was eliminated because I spelled the word "earnest" wrong. I will always remember the right way to spell it for the rest of my life.

ALL ABOUT VICTORIA

- Victoria's fave subject is English — "I love reading, creative writing, and spelling."
- Victoria's fave books are the Twilight series, and the author Stephenie Myer is her favorite, too.
- Victoria takes Spanish in school.

TAYLOR LAUTNER

SPORTY STUDENT

Taylor Lautner has been acting since he was nine years old, but in school he was much more well-known for his athletic attitude than his acting skills!

Public School . . . Taylor went to public school until his acting schedule became too hectic for him to keep up. "I tried to stay in school as long as I could. I went to a public school my whole life until this year."

According to Taylor's dad, Dan . . . "Because of all that's happening for him, we want him to do normal things. We kept him in public school as long as we could, so he could be with his peers. We give him responsibilities at home — chores he has to do. He gets an allotted allowance and he has to budget it."

Football star . . . The one thing Taylor misses most about public school is playing on the football team. "I played football my whole life and had to give it up last year because I had to miss too many practices and it was kind of rough for me. It is kind of hard watching the high school football games now. I played running back and slot receiver and strong safety on defense."

May I Have This Dance? . . .

Taylor isn't afraid to get out on the dance floor and show off his moves! "At my school, juniors and seniors both go to the prom. It was fun. I forget where we had it; it was somewhere in LA at some art museum. It was really a lot of fun. It was a long night. I think it finished like twelve or one in the morning."

Little Known Fact . . .

Taylor was trouble when he first began school. "I was a biter at day care. I don't remember it, but my parents tell me I'd bite other kids."

DEMI LOVATO

School Days Memories

You might say Demi Lovato is on the fast track to success. She burst onto the scene as the Jonas Brothers' costar in *Camp Rock*. Only months after that, she released her first CD, *Don't Forget*, got her own TV series, *Sonny With a Chance*, and signed up for *Camp Rock 2*. Of course, there's the fact that she's a buddy of Nick, Joe, and Kevin Jonas — now that's the tip-top in itself!

But what about Demi's earlier days . . . when she was back in school? Well, it wasn't all fun and games. Take a peek at Demi's school days blog!

"FRENEMIES" . . .

"I think [getting backstabbed by a friend] is part of growing up. There were these girls I dealt with at school who I thought were my best friends, who just turned on me, and that made it really hard. . . . They were just being bullies. There were several times where I would call my mom, crying, and say, 'Please take me out of school!' . . . They were threatening to me. One day the popular girls wrote a hate letter, a petition, which said, 'If anyone hates Demi, sign this letter.' And it got passed around school. Everyone who wanted to be popular signed it."

DEMI'S BOOK LIST

- "*The Diary of Anne Frank* and *The Pearl* — they are classics everyone should read. I like the metaphors in *The Pearl*, and the story behind *Anne Frank* opens up your heart."
- "My favorite books as a child were *Brindle*, *I'll Love You Forever*, and *Junie B. Jones*."
- "The first book I read myself was *The Very Hungry Caterpillar*."

CODY LINLEY

LOL School Tales

Everyone knows that *Hannah Montana's* Cody Linley is a fun kind of guy. He's always cracking up his *HM* cast-mates, and he put a smile on all the dancing couples' faces when he competed on *Dancing with the Stars*. He even caused the giggles on the set of his movie *The Haunting Hour!* Well, anyone who's known Cody since he was a little guy back in Texas isn't surprised. He was definitely known as Mr. Happy-Go-Lucky back at school. Here are a few of his grin-worthy memories. . .

Cody Clips

- Cody's fave book series was R. L. Stine's Goosebumps — he still has all the books!
- Cody attended Degan Elementary School in Denton, TX.
- Cody's fave day of the week is Friday — "Even though you have to go to school, it's the best feeling ever when you get out at the end of a Friday. You've got a huge weekend ahead of you!"

YAKKER: "I was always the class clown. The teachers say I usually talk a little too much!"

MATH WIZ: "I like math. It's probably one of my strongest subjects in school. I like it because it's challenging, and it's really, really helpful in life. You use math all the time, every single day. There's so much you need math for. I like to look at a huge equation, complete it, and know I got the right answer. It's a good sense of accomplishment."

B-BOY: "I played basketball — point guard — in middle school and high school."

LITTLE DRUMMER BOY: "I used to get in trouble in school all the time for drumming. I guess it can be pretty annoying. I still get in trouble for it with my mom. It's so weird; I can't even control it. It's not like I do it on purpose. The music is just inside of me, and it's got to be let out somehow."

OOPS! "My most embarrassing moment in school was in art class in sixth grade. A girl pulled out a chair from underneath me right before I sat down, and I hit the ground. I don't know why, but it left an impression, everyone laughing at me. Usually I laugh at myself in that kind of situation, but I was in pain. I did not think it was funny at all. Everyone was laughing at me."

TAYLOR SWIFT

Country's Teen Queen

Believe it or not, at 19, award-winning country singer Taylor Swift has lots of life experiences to sing and write about! They may not be adult topics, but all her songs touch on her personal real-life heartaches, breaks, and throbs! Her debut CD, *Taylor Swift*, zoomed right up the country and pop charts, as did her second effort, *Fearless*. When asked if there is a song on either CD that has special meaning to her, Taylor admits she really can't pick just one, but the song "The Outside" from *Taylor Swift* explains what lots of kids go through in school every day.

Taylor wrote "The Outside" when she was 12 years old. It's all about rejection and being on the outside. "I think it happens to everybody at some point in her life, where you're completely on the outside of things," she explains. "It happened to me . . . in the seventh grade. I'd been best friends with this group of girls for as long as I could remember, but all of a sudden, they were cool and I wasn't anymore. I didn't look as cool or act as cool as they did, and I couldn't figure out why they didn't want to hang out with me anymore. And that was really sad, to sit there and wonder, 'What's wrong with me?'

"I remember when I called those girls early in the day and was like, 'Hey you guys want to go to the mall?' And they were like, 'Oh, no, I've got plans' or 'I'm gonna stay home.' Everyone had a different excuse. So my mom and I went to the mall — and we ran into them hanging out together in a store! I just remember my mom saying, 'We're going to the King of Prussia Mall!' which is the best mall in the whole state. . . . She let me run from my pain for a little bit, and I thought that was the nicest thing that she ever could have done."